Sassy Southern Classy Cajun

Sylvia Dickey Smith

Eat Southern food!

Sylvia Dickey Smith

Cover and Interior Design by L & L Dreamspell

Copyright © 2009 Sylvia Dickey Smith. All rights reserved. No part of this publication may be reproduced, stored in a retrieval system or transmitted in any form or by any means, electronic, mechanical, photocopying, recording or otherwise without the prior written permission of the copyright holder, except for brief quotations used in a review.

ISBN: 978-1-60318-174-7

Visit us on the web at www.lldreamspell.com

Published by L & L Dreamspell
Printed in the United States of America

Table of Contents

APPETIZERS
- Benedictine Spread — 10
- Boudain Dip — 10
- Cajun Bowties — 11
- Cajun Pinwheels — 11
- Orange, Texas Party Punch — 12
- Shrimp Mold — 12
- Swamp Dip — 13

BREADS
- Apple Cornbread — 16
- Banana Bread — 17
- Brazil Nut Bread — 18
- Buckskin Bread — 19
- Sassy Southern Cornbread — 20

BREAKFAST
- Bluebird Omelet — 22
- Breakfast Casserole — 23
- Russ' Granola — 24

DESSERTS
- Blueberry Pie — 26
- Easy-Peezy Blueberry Pie — 26
- Bread Puddin' — 27
- Buttermilk Pie — 28
- Coconut Pineapple Pie — 29
- Creole Pecan Pralines — 30
- Green Tomato Pie — 31
- Jeff Davis Pie — 32
- No Fail Fudge — 33
- Peanut Butter Fudge — 34

Peanut Pattie Candy	35
Pecan Cobbler	36
Pecan Toffee Candy	37
Peggy's Iron Skillet Chocolate Pie	38
Pistachio Bark Candy	39
Praline Cookies	40
Rice Pudding	41
Sheri's Decadent Chocolate Cookies	42
Southern Hot Milk Cake	44
Stratigrafy Candy	46
Tea Cakes	48

MAIN DISHES

Aunt Annie's Dirty Rice	50
Aunt Annie's Chicken & Dumplings	50
Authentic Northeast Louisiana Cajun Gumbo	52
Bayou Blend	53
Cajun Gumbo For Texans	54
Cajun Jambalaya	56
Cheese Button Casserole	57
Cheese Enchiladas	58
Chicken Gumbo	60
Chicken Soup Extraordinaire	60
Chicken Tetrazini	61
Chili Tamale Casserole	62
Chipolte Burgers	63
Cornbread Dressing	64
Crawfish Cornbread	65
Crawfish Etouffe	66
Crawfish Pie	66
Crawfish Soup	68
Eggplant and Shrimp Casserole	69
Fried Catfish	70
Fried Shrimp	72
Grillades	73

I Don't Know	74
Meat Enchiladas	75
Russ' Chili: A Work in Progress	76
Seafood Casserole	78
Smothered Chicken	79
Southern Fried Chicken	80
Another Version of Southern Fried Chicken	81
Seafood Stuffed Chinese Cabbage	82
Texas Barbeque Dammit	83
Barbeque Ribs	84
"Wright" Stew	85

VEGETABLES

Aunt Annie's Corn Patties	88
Broccoli Salad	88
Cajun Potato Salad	89
Christmas Carrots	89
Coleslaw	90
Corn Casserole	91
Extra Crispy Cajun Fry Batter	92
Family Favorite Potato Salad	92
Fried Green Tomatoes	93
Fried Okra	93
Onion Pie	94
Pinto Beans and More	95
Red Grape & Broccoli Salad	96
Southern Sweet Potato Crisp	96
Sweet Potato Casserole	97
Swiss Chard & White Beans	98
Tamale Mashed Potatoes	98

BONUS RECIPE

Sidra Smart's Sassy Pickles	99

Dedicated to my mother, Ruth Thomas Dickey
Sept. 2, 1918 - Feb. 24, 2008

A woman who loved her children, southern cooking, good-looking men, dancing, and beautiful music, not necessarily in that order.

Preface

The term, *Sassy Southern—Classy Cajun* may sound like an oxymoron to the average person, but in southeast Texas where southerners and Cajuns all sleep under the same threat of hurricanes and where mosquitoes grow big as dragonflies, good food is the common denominator. Gregarious folks welcome any excuse to get together for fellowship, fun and lively music.

One Sidra Smart fan, says, "Cooking is home, Momma's kitchen, where everyone gathers, where aromas bring back precious memories of the family sitting around the table talking and waiting for the gumbo to get finished, eating crackers with Tabasco Sauce poured on them and raw oysters out of the jar, the juice dripping down your chin. You can't wait for that first taste of the simmering pot of goodness, Christmas tree lights glittering on the tree in the corner of the living room. Good food brings families home to love."

Another says, "Cooking brings home to wherever you are. We moved five times when I was a kid. The only thing that stayed the same was my mother's special dishes. Passion and comfort. Reassurance and recognition. I remember her stuffed peppers on a winter day—how warm it made me feel, inside and out."

No wonder Sidra Smart has fallen in love with the area, the people, and the food. She offers a sampling of a few great recipes. And in the end, shares her famous *Sassy Pickles* recipe.

RECIPE WINNERS

Cajun 1ˢᵗ Place—Betty Davis—***Cajun Potato Salad***
Runner up—Tommye Johnson—***Boudain Dip***

Southern 1ˢᵗ Place—Doris Bethard—***Tea Cakes***
Runner up—John Browning—***Bluebird Omelet***

Thank you to all the people who contributed recipes. Remember that Sylvia's friends and family members were not eligible for the drawing—we're sorry about that… Also note that some of the entries were missing a name—so please excuse us if your name was left off.

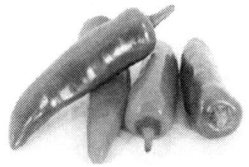

APPETIZERS

"Boy, you've bitten' off more than you can chew."

Recipe on page 12

BENEDICTINE SPREAD
By Lyn Baldwin

1 8 ounce package softened cream cheese
1 large cucumber peeled and seeded
¼ teaspoon salt, or to taste
¼ teaspoon garlic powder
1 - 2 drops green food coloring (optional)
Cooked bacon strips, crumbled

Process peeled, seeded cucumber until mushy. Drain well on paper towel.
Process cream cheese, add onion salt, garlic powder and food coloring and then add cucumber.
Process until well mixed.
Sprinkle bacon on top. Serve with fresh bread or crackers.

Boudain DIP
By Tommye Johnson

2 lbs boudain
16 oz. sour cream

Remove boudain from casing; mix with sour cream. Serve with crackers or crudités.

CAJUN BOWTIES

1 package of bowtie pasta
Cajun seasoning
Oil

Cook bowtie pasta in boiling water until tender.
Drain, wiping off most of water.
Drop by bowties into hot oil and fry until brown, remove and place on a platter covered with paper towels and sprinkle with Cajun seasoning while still hot. Cool and enjoy. A great snack for a party.

CAJUN PINWHEELS

8 oz. package cream cheese, softened
Dash of salt and pepper
½ teaspoon cayenne pepper
¼ cup black olives, chopped
¼ cup green olives, chopped
2 Tablespoons finely chopped onion
1 cup Monterrey Jack cheese, shredded
1 pound cooked salad shrimp, chopped
7 flour tortillas

Combine cream cheese, salt, pepper, spices, olives, onion, cheese and shrimp in a small bowl. Stir well, spread over tortillas and then roll tightly. Cover with plastic wrap and chill in refrigerator at least two hours. Slice rolls ½ inch thick and layer on platter.

ORANGE, TEXAS PARTY PUNCH
By Ann Pence

1 ½ pints Orange Juice
1 ½ quarts White Grape Juice
1 quart Ginger Ale
1 fifth Smirnoff Vodka

Stir altogether in punch bowl with large chunks of ice. Garnish with Orange slices and mint leaves.

SHRIMP MOLD

1 can tomato soup
1 - 8 ounce package cream cheese
1½ Tablespoons Knox gelatin
1 cup mayonnaise
¾ cup finely chopped celery
¾ cup finely chopped onions
1 can shrimp or freshly cooked shrimp
Salt & pepper to taste

Soak gelatin in 1¼ cups cold water. Heat soup to boiling, add cream cheese and dissolve thoroughly then mix with gelatin. Cool. Add mayonnaise, celery, salt and pepper. When it begins to thicken, add shrimp and pour into fish-shaped mold if possible. Set until firm; place in fridge covered with waxed paper.
Unmold and serve with crackers.

SWAMP DIP
By Ann Pence

4 cans (15 ounce) Ranch Style Beans, mashed

Add
½ cup butter
½ pound sharp cheese, grated
2 Jalapeno peppers, cut finely
1 onion, medium, chopped finely
2 cloves of fresh garlic, chopped finely

Mix in top of double boiler. Cook until blended. Best if done in chafing dish and kept warm.

Sassy Southern—Classy Cajun

BREADS

"He knows what side his bread's buttered on."

Recipe on page 20

APPLE CORNBREAD

2 packages Jiffy Corn Muffin Mix
½ cup sugar
1 Tablespoon cinnamon
3 eggs
1 Tablespoon oil
½ teaspoon vanilla

Mix together and gently fold in:
1 can apple pie filling

Pour in greased pan, bake at 350°F for 30 minutes or until golden brown. While still hot, sprinkle with sugar and cinnamon. Delicious, especially when served with a scoop of vanilla ice cream.

BANANA BREAD
By Glenda Dickey

5 Tablespoons butter
½ cup sugar
½ cup brown sugar
1 egg
2 egg whites (or you can use two eggs)
1 teaspoon vanilla
1 ½ cups mashed bananas
1 ¾ cups flour
1 teaspoon baking soda
½ teaspoon salt
¼ teaspoon baking powder
½ cup evaporated milk or cream
1/3 cup chopped nuts (pecans or walnuts are best)

Mix butter, sugar, and brown sugar. Add eggs, vanilla, and mashed bananas. Mix dry ingredients together and add to earlier mixture alternating with the cream. Stir in nuts.

Pour into greased loaf pan and bake at 350°F for 1 hour. Or, if preferred, 1 hour 15 minutes at 325°F.

BRAZIL NUT BREAD

2 cups chopped Brazil Nuts
2 – 8 ounce packages pitted chopped dates
1 cup chopped pecans
1 cup chopped maraschino cherries
¾ cup flour
¾ cup sugar
½ teaspoon baking powder
½ teaspoon salt
3 eggs, beaten
1 teaspoon vanilla

Combine first 4 ingredients; stir well. Combine dry ingredients. Stir into fruit mixture. Add eggs and vanilla and mix well. Spoon batter into a greased and waxed paper lined loaf pan. Bake at 300°F for 1 hour 45 minutes or until wooden pick inserted in center comes out clean. Cool in pan 10 minutes. Remove from pan and cool completely. Yield: One loaf.

BUCKSKIN BREAD
By Marian Allen

Simple, but good. My whole family loves this stuff. At first, it's only good with soup/stew, but then it's addictive. Adapted from an American Indian Cooking cookbook.

2 cups self-rising flour

1 cup water

Mix, pat the dough into a ball, pat it with olive oil, put it on a greased cookie sheet and bake at 400°F for about 20 minutes. Serve warm with butter or soup/stew.

SASSY SOUTHERN CORNBREAD
By Glenda Dickey

1 cup white corn meal
1 cup flour
1 teaspoon salt
2 rounded Tablespoons baking powder
2 Tablespoons sugar
Buttermilk (approximately 1 cup)

Combine all ingredients and mix. Batter should be the consistency of a heavy cake batter. Pour 2 to 3 Tablespoons oil in skillet. Pour in batter—any oil that seeps up, spoon on top of batter. Bake in skillet at 425°F until brown. (Yes, this recipe does *not* contain eggs.)

BREAKFAST

"Well, butter my biscuit."

Recipe on page 24

BLUEBIRD OMELET
By John Browning

½ cup celery, diced small
¼ cup green bell pepper, diced small
¼ cup red bell pepper, diced course
1 cup onion, diced small
2 cups diced Irish potatoes, unpeeled, well-scrubbed, eyes and blemishes carved out, diced into ¼ inch squares
1 cup Colby Jack cheese, diced small
8 extra-large or 10 large eggs, well-beaten
1 Tablespoon garlic, diced small
½ to 1½ teaspoons salt
1/3 to ½ teaspoon paprika
1/3 to ½ teaspoon basil
1/3 to ½ teaspoon black pepper
¼ or less teaspoon red pepper
1/3 cup olive oil
½ to 1 cup Chablis wine

You will need a large frying pan, 10" or greater, or equivalent. Dice the celery, bell peppers, onion, potatoes, and garlic and mix well in a large bowl. Dice the cheese and set aside in a separate container.

Into the large frying pan pour the olive oil and heat it medium-high. Pour in the mixed vegetables and cook until the potato is just translucent and not a bit longer, stirring gently often. Pour in enough wine to cradle, not submerge the food and season to taste. Turn the heat down to simmer and simmer for about 15 minutes. Beat the eggs while the food is simmering.

Turn the heat up to a low setting such as you would use to bake a pancake and stir in the beaten eggs and diced cheese. Cook until the eggs are just done, stirring often, remove from heat and cover until served.

Goes great with sausage, bacon or pork, and fruit.
Serves 4.

BREAKFAST CASSEROLE
By Carolyn West

7 to 8 eggs, beaten
1 pound Jimmy Dean Hot Sausage
1 package Grated Sharp Cheddar Cheese
1 small can chopped green chilies
½ cup chopped black olives
2 cans crescent rolls
Salt and pepper to taste

Crumble and fry sausage in skillet.

Roll out one can of crescent rolls and place in a 9 x 12 inch baking dish (without separating).

Spread sausage over rolls in bottom of dish.

Mix eggs, chilies, olives, salt and pepper and carefully pour over rolls in dish.

Add cheese.

Carefully roll out second can of crescent rolls and place on top, pressing around sides.

Bake at 325°F approx. 50 minutes.

Test center for doneness.

RUSS'S GRANOLA
By Russell Thomas Hogg

3 cups rolled oats or steel-cut oats
1 cup slivered/sliced almonds
1 cup walnuts or pecans
½ cup wheat germ
1/3 cup maple syrup (a variation is Steen's Pure Cane Syrup)
1/3 cup olive oil (or lighter oil, if desired)
½ teaspoon ground cinnamon
Dash or two of salt

Preheat oven to 225°F. Mix nuts and grains together with cinnamon; stir together oil and syrup with salt, then stir the two mixtures together.

Spread out on a baking sheet and place in the oven stirring every twenty to thirty minutes until the granola achieves a light golden color (about 1¼ to 1½ hours). Cool and store in an airtight container.

NOTE: This is my favorite way to make this recipe, but you can do any number of variations; it's very flexible. You can use honey instead of syrup, can use nutmeg or cinnamon, can substitute or add any nuts you want, and can add dried fruit like raisins. Good served with milk or yogurt for breakfast; makes a good trail mix if you add M&M's. Now I hardly ever buy cereal for myself anymore.

DESSERTS

"We just been chewin' the fat."

Recipe on page 33

BLUEBERRY PIE

1 graham cracker crust
Topping: Make and set aside
2 cups blueberries
½ cup water
1 Tablespoon corn starch
¼ cup Splenda

Cook until thick and clear then add:
½ teaspoon fresh lemon juice
Cool to room temperature

Filling:
Blend 4 ounces reduced fat cream cheese
1 Tablespoon sugar
¼ cup Splenda
Stir in 8 ounces sugar free Cool Whip

Pour into the graham cracker crust then spoon cooled topping on top.

EASY-PEEZY BLUEBERRY PIE

1 - 12 ounce package Cool Whip
1 - 8 ounce package cream cheese
1 can sweetened condensed cream
1/3 cup lemon juice

Mix all together then add fresh blueberries. Pour into graham cracker crust or baked pie shell.

BREAD PUDDIN'

2 cups sugar
5 large eggs
1 cup water + 1 cup evaporated milk, combined
2 teaspoons vanilla
3 cups Italian bread, cut and allowed to stale overnight in a bowl
1 cup packed light brown sugar
¼ cup butter, softened
1 cup pecans, chopped

Grease a 13 x 9 x 2 inch pan. Mix together granulated sugar, eggs, and milk in a bowl; add vanilla. Pour over cubed bread and let sit for 10 minutes. In another bowl, mix and crumble together brown sugar, butter and pecans. Pour bread mixture into prepared pan. Sprinkle brown sugar mixture over the top and bake for 35 to 45 minutes at 350°F or until set. Remove from oven.

Whisky/Brandy Sauce for topping

1 cup sugar
½ cup butter
1 egg, beaten
2 teaspoons vanilla
¼ cup Whisky or Brandy

Mix together sugar, butter, egg and vanilla in a saucepan. Over medium heat, stir together until sugar is melted. Add Whisky or Brandy, stirring well. Pour over bread pudding. Delicious served warm or cold.

BUTTERMILK PIE

No southern cookbook is complete without a recipe for buttermilk pie. Don't worry if you don't like the taste of buttermilk, because this pie doesn't taste like it.

1 stick melted butter
1 ¾ cups sugar
3 Tablespoons flour
3 eggs, beaten
1 teaspoon vanilla
½ teaspoon freshly grated nutmeg
¼ teaspoon salt
1 cup buttermilk
1 unbaked pie shell

Combine butter, sugar, flour, eggs, buttermilk, vanilla, nutmeg and salt in a large bowl and whisk until smooth.

Pour mixture in pie crust and bake 45 to 50 minutes in oven preheated to 350°F.
Cool on wire rack and refrigerate until ready to serve.

COCONUT PINEAPPLE PIE
By Oda Hudgins

1 cup sugar
3 Tablespoons flour
1 cup white corn syrup
1 cup grated coconut
1 - 8 ounce can crushed pineapple, undrained
3 eggs, beaten
1 teaspoon vanilla extract
1 unbaked pie shell
¼ cup melted butter
Chopped pecans

In a bowl, combine sugar and flour, then add corn syrup, coconut, pineapple, eggs and vanilla. Drizzle with butter. Sprinkle on chopped pecans.
Bake at 350°F until knife comes out clean.
Cool on wire rack.
Chill before serving.

CREOLE PECAN PRALINES

1 cup brown sugar
2 cups granulated sugar
1 cup water
1/16 teaspoon salt
1 teaspoon vanilla
3 cups pecan halves
2 Tablespoons butter

Mix sugar and water in a deep iron skillet or a copper kettle and heat until it boils. Add the pecans. Continue to cook, stirring gently over a low fire until the mixture will grain when tested by rubbing the back of the spoon against the side of the skillet—240°F. Plant the seed crystals thus formed into the mixture, repeating 3 or 4 times. Remove from fire. Add salt, butter and vanilla and continue to stir until the syrup will adhere to the nuts when poured by spoonful on waxed paper. When cold remove from paper. Individual ones or pralinettes may be made by using a teaspoon to drip them. Place a piece of plain paper under the waxed paper before pouring the pralines.

If the mixture gets hard before you finish pouring, you can add a little water and cook to boiling again then pour the rest of the pralines. This recipe makes between 70 and 80 pecan pralines.

This is the original recipe from the Godchaux Sugar Company. These are authentic tasting pralines and this is how pralines were made in the 1800s. Today, pralines are made with milk and do not taste the same.

GREEN TOMATO PIE

6 cups thinly sliced green tomatoes (approximately 2 pounds)
1 cup sugar
3 Tablespoons flour
2 teaspoons finely shredded lemon peel
3 Tablespoons lemon juice
2 Tablespoons melted butter
¼ teaspoon salt
¼ teaspoon grated nutmeg
¼ teaspoon cinnamon
Pinch of ground cloves

Place tomatoes in large bowl. Pour boiling water over to cover and let stand for 20 minutes, then drain.

In small bowl, combine sugar, lemon juice, lemon peel, butter, salt and spices. Add mixture to tomatoes, stir to combine.

Pour in pastry lined pie plate. Cut strips from a second pie crust and lattice across the top of pie.

Bake at 450°F for 10 minutes, reduce heat to 375°F and bake 35 to 40 minutes or until bubbly. Cool on wire rack.

JEFF DAVIS PIE

A true southern recipe that is delicious and easy to make.

½ cup butter
2 cups sugar
1 Tablespoon flour
¼ teaspoon salt
1 teaspoon vanilla
4 eggs
1 cup milk
1 unbaked pie shell

Cream together butter and sugar until light and fluffy then add flour, salt, vanilla, and beat well. Add eggs one at a time beating well after each addition. Slowly stir in milk.

Pour into well chilled shell. Bake at 450°F for 10 minutes. Reduce heat to 350°F and continue baking for 30 minutes or until firm.

NO FAIL FUDGE

Old-fashioned candy at its best.

2 cups sugar
3 Tablespoons unsweetened cocoa powder
½ cup evaporated milk
1/3 cup white Karo syrup
2 Tablespoons butter
1 teaspoon vanilla
Pecans (optional)

Mix all together in a large saucepan and bring to complete rolling boil and time for exactly three minutes, stirring constantly. Cool and beat until thick and pour in buttered plate. Cool and cut in squares. For variety, stir in a tablespoon or two of peanut butter before beating. Yum!

PEANUT BUTTER FUDGE

A Christmas Favorite.

2 cups sugar
1 small can (2/3 cup) evaporated milk
1 pinch of salt
10 large marshmallows
1 stick of butter
6 ounces peanut butter chips

Combine sugar, milk and salt and stir well. Add the marshmallows and cook in a large saucepan over a slow fire until it begins to boil, stirring constantly. Once it comes to a full rolling boil set the timer for 6 minutes. When the 6 minutes are up remove from the fire and add the butter and the peanut butter chips. Stir till all melts and spread on a buttered dish to cool. Once cool cut into small squares. Keep in refrigerator. For variety, substitute semi-sweet chocolate chips, or white chocolate chips for peanut butter chips.

PEANUT PATTIE CANDY

3 cups sugar
1 cup water
1 cup White Karo Syrup
3 cups raw peanuts
½ teaspoon Red food coloring
½ stick butter
pinch of salt
1/3 cup sifted powdered sugar

Bring sugar, water and syrup to a boil. Add raw peanuts and red food coloring. Cook to hard ball state (260°F). Remove from heat and add butter, salt & powdered sugar. Beat in pot with electric mixer until really stiff. Pour out on buttered cookie sheet or large 9x13 pan as fast as you can. When cool break apart or cut with a knife. It is easier to break than cut.

Results: The ultimate, most supreme, superior, wonderful, pure ecstasy, yummy for the tummy all time favorite of a couple of grandkids, and Granny Sylvia.

PECAN COBBLER

3 cups flour
1 cup butter
1/2 to 3/4 cup cream
3 cups pecans
1 teaspoon cinnamon
1 cup sugar
½ cup water
1 Tablespoon baking powder
1 teaspoon salt

Bring the water to a boil. Add the sugar, and cook to the softball stage. Remove from the heat, and beat in ½ cup butter, then 1 cup flour, and the cinnamon. Mix in the pecans, and spread in the bottom of a greased baking dish.

Preheat the oven to 400°F. Cut the remaining flour into the remaining butter until it is very granular. Add the baking powder and salt, and mix in by tossing. Using a fork, mix in the cream, a little at a time until the mixture is just shy of pourable. Drop by spoonfuls onto the pecans.

Immediately place in oven. After 15 minutes, reduce heat to 350°F and bake for another 30 minutes, or until filling bubbles up.

Delicious served with Blue Bell Homemade Vanilla ice cream! (But isn't anything better served with Blue Bell?!)

PECAN TOFFEE CANDY
By Trish Stuart

2 cups sugar
2 cups butter (no substitutes)

Cook in heavy saucepan over medium heat until it comes to a rolling boil, turning amber. Temperature should be 285°F when done. Remember to stir often!

Meanwhile, butter a shallow cookie sheet. Sprinkle 1 cup chopped pecans over buttered pan. Chop a cup or two of milk chocolate and set aside.

Pour sugar/butter toffee over pecans.

Sprinkle chocolate over top and spread with spatula as it melts. Sprinkle more pecans on top for "prettiness." Let it cool. Break apart.

PEGGY'S IRON SKILLET CHOCOLATE PIE
By Peggy McAdams

Bake one pie shell according to your favorite recipe or package directions and put aside.

In small bowl add 2 heaping teaspoons flour, mixed with 2 teaspoons Hershey's Cocoa.

Add two egg yolks to one cup of milk and mix well.

In a large iron skillet, melt 2 Tablespoons margarine or butter, add dry ingredients, then add milk/egg mixture. Stir until thick. Add 1 teaspoon vanilla. Pour into baked pie shell and top with meringue and bake at 375°F until light brown.

Be sure to use an iron skillet and make only one pie at the time.

PISTACHIO BARK CANDY
By Julie Vasek

12 ounces semi sweet chocolate
¾ cup dried, sweet cranberries
1 cup white chocolate
1 cup pistachios, salted

Toast nuts on baking sheet in 350°F oven for maybe 10 minutes—watch that they don't burn.

Melt dark chocolate in glass dish or measuring cup in microwave at ½ power for 1 ½ minutes, stir, cook another 1 ½ minutes on half power, stir, repeat a third time until melted.

Add ½ of the nuts and cranberries.

Meanwhile, melt white chocolate the same way as the dark chocolate. Spread on cookie sheet. Drop melted white chocolate by tablespoons into the other mixture. Use bread knife to blend lightly. Scatter remaining nuts and cranberry mixture over chocolate and pat in.

Refrigerate for an hour or until hard.

Cut or break into pieces.

PRALINE COOKIES

1 egg white, stiffly beaten
1 cup brown sugar
2 Tablespoons flour
1 teaspoon vanilla extract
2 cups chopped pecans

Mix all ingredients well. Place by spoonful on parchment paper or greased foil.
Bake at 275°F for 30 minutes. Leave on cookie sheet until cool then remove to wire rack.
Makes approximately 15 cookies.

RICE PUDDING
By Glenda Dickey

1 cup sugar
3 eggs, beaten
1½ cups cooked rice
½ stick melted butter
1 teaspoon vanilla
2 cups milk (or you may use 1 cup evaporated milk and 1 cup water)

Combine ingredients and bake in buttered baking dish at 350 °F for 45 minutes.

SHERI'S DECADENT CHOCOLATE COOKIES

1 cup chopped pecans
12 ounces dark chocolate (I use Ghirardelli Bittersweet Chocolate Bars)
12 ounces semi-sweet chocolate chips
2 cups Quaker Oats
2 cups all purpose flour
1 teaspoon baking powder
1 teaspoon baking soda
½ teaspoon salt
½ pound Blue Bonnet Margarine (2 sticks) softened
1 cup dark brown sugar
1 cup granulated sugar
2 eggs
1 ½ teaspoons vanilla extract
OPTIONAL INGREDIENT: 1 cup dried tart cherries. I use Rainier cherries from www.chukar.com

Preheat oven to 350 °F. Butter cookie sheets or use parchment paper.

In a nonstick pan, toast pecans over medium-low heat, stirring constantly for about 10 to 15 minutes. Turn out onto a plate to cool.

Chop chocolate bar into small chunks.

In a large mixing bowl, beat the butter until creamy. Add sugars and beat until light and fluffy, about 4 minutes. Add the eggs and vanilla. Beat the mixture until well combined, about a minute. Add the dry ingredients to the mixture and beat at low speed until well combined, less than a minute. Add chocolate chips, chopped chocolate, cherries and nuts. Use a sturdy wooden spoon, mix well by hand, until all the ingredients are thoroughly incorporated.

Scoop by tablespoon, measure out cookies on sheets, leaving 2 inches between cookies (about a dozen per sheet). Bake 12 to 14 minutes, or until the cookies have set and are slightly flattened and light brown. Cool on sheets 2 minutes, then transfer to racks to cool completely. Yield 5 to 6 dozen.

SOUTHERN HOT MILK CAKE
By Carol Staggs

4 eggs
2 cups sugar
2 cups flour
1 cup milk
½ stick butter
1 teaspoon baking powder
1 teaspoon vanilla extract

Heat milk and butter in saucepan till butter is melted.
Beat eggs in mixing bowl until fluffy.
Add sugar and beat into eggs.
Add flour gradually to sugar and egg mixture.
Pour in hot milk and butter and beat till creamy.
Add baking powder and vanilla and beat until mixed.
Pour into greased Bundt pan.
Bake at 350° F and bake for 50-55 minutes until toothpick comes out clean.

STRATIGRAFY CANDY
By Russell Thomas Hogg

Bottom Layer
1 cup (6 ounces) milk chocolate chips
¼ cup butterscotch chips
¼ cup creamy peanut butter

Filling
¼ cup butter or margarine
1 cup sugar
¼ cup evaporated milk
1½ cups marshmallow cream
¼ cup creamy peanut butter
1 teaspoon vanilla extract
1½ cups chopped salted peanuts

Caramel layer
1 package (14 ounces) caramels
¼ cup whipping cream

Icing
1 cup (6 ounces) milk chocolate chips
¼ cup butterscotch chips
¼ cup creamy peanut butter

Combine the first three ingredients in a small saucepan; stir over low heat until melted and smooth. Spread onto the bottom of a lightly greased 13x9x2 inch pan. Refrigerate until set.

For filling, melt butter in a heavy saucepan over medium high heat. Add sugar and milk. Bring to a boil; boil and stir for 5 minutes. Remove from the heat; stir in marshmallow cream, peanut butter and vanilla. Add peanuts. Spread over 1st layer. Refrigerate until set.

Combine the caramels and cream in a saucepan; stir over low heat until melted and smooth. Spread over the filling. Refrigerate until set.

In another saucepan, combine chips and peanut butter; stir over low heat until melted and smooth. Pour over the caramel layer. Refrigerate for at least 1 hour. Cut into 1 inch squares. Store in refrigerator.

These are spectacular!

TEA CAKES

By Doris Bethard—1985 (Recipe at that time was over 100 years old, when asked where the recipe came from she could not remember who she had gotten it from.)

2 cups sugar
1 cup unsalted butter or Crisco (I use butter for better flavor)
1 teaspoon baking soda
4 eggs
1/3 cup clabber or buttermilk
Enough all purpose flour to make stiff dough (approximately 3 ½ cups)

Mix all ingredients together. Place in greased glass bowl and place in refrigerator for at least 4 hours before cutting. Roll out dough on pastry sheet dusted with flour. Roll dough to about ¼ inch thick or the thickness of your choice. Dust cookie cutters with flour before cutting out cookies. Place cookies on parchment paper and bake at 375°F for 15 to 20 minutes.

Cool on cookie sheet for 2 minutes then remove to cooling rack. Cool completely and frost.

Frosting

Powdered sugar
Water
Food coloring

Mix powdered sugar with small bits of water adding food coloring for desired colors. Mixture should be almost as thick as peanut butter. If it is too runny it will not stay on the cookie.

MAIN DISHES

"Don't count your chickens before they hatch."

Recipe on page 50

AUNT ANNIE'S DIRTY RICE

1 pound ground beef
1 pound of ground pork
½ onion, chopped
1 small bell pepper, chopped
1 cup water
1 small head of cabbage, chopped
Salt, Black pepper, Red pepper
4 cups cooked rice

Brown beef and pork in a large skillet. Add water, onion and bell pepper and cook for approximately 10 minutes. Add cabbage and season with salt and peppers. Stir well and cover. Turn fire to medium and cook 20 to 25 minutes, stirring often. Add about 4 cups cooked rice and stir well. Season to taste. Lower heat and simmer about 10 minutes, stirring often, to let the seasoning go through the rice.

AUNT ANNIE'S CHICKEN & DUMPLINGS

Aunt Annie was proud of her chicken and dumplings. She always browned her hen, adding water when needed and the broth was a rich brown that she then cooked her dumplings in. They were really good but she thought everyone else's dumplings were not good because they were those "sickly white dumplings."

2-3 pieces of chicken
2 cans chicken broth
Flour for dusting
Salt & Pepper

Creole Seasoning
Garlic
1-2 cans cream of chicken soup, optional

Sauté onions in some oil, then add chicken to brown (whole chicken or legs). Add a little water. Brown the chicken down again until the water disappears then add a little more water. Repeat this step about 5 to 6 times. (This is the part that takes a while to master, but the browning of the chicken gives the dumplings a great taste).

Add approximately 4 cups of water and chicken broth. Add salt, pepper and Creole seasoning to taste. Simmer until tender; stew should be dark from browned chicken. Remove chicken. Let cool to touch and shred chicken back into broth.

TO MAKE DUMPLINGS
3 cups flour
1 egg
1 tsp baking powder
1 tsp shortening
1 tsp salt
Milk (add till you get the right consistency)

Combine all dry ingredients. Add egg and milk and mix until you get the right consistency and form into a ball. Add a light layer of flour around the ball to keep it from sticking to your hands.

Roll out dumplings and cut into 1-inch squares and drop into hot mixture. Boil for 10 minutes or until dumplings are cooked. Stir occasionally. Flour from dumplings should thicken the stew. (Sometimes I add cream of chicken soup to help thicken the mixture, but Aunt Annie would be horrified).

AUTHENTIC NORTHEAST LOUISIANA CAJUN GUMBO

In a large black cast iron skillet pour cooking oil and add flour. The amount will vary based on how much you want to make. A good "rule of thumb" is to start out with approximately one cup of cooking oil then gauge the amount of flour by the consistency as you are adding. The consistency should be very stiff, but easy to stir while browning over medium to high heat. Just remember that once the browning begins it is easy to burn and you do not want a burned taste. You must stir constantly until the browning process is complete. When the roux is the color of a dark old copper penny, it is ready. Another hint: you can turn off the fire a little before it is almost brown enough and it will continue to brown in the hot iron skillet. Also, if it is dark enough and you do not want it any browner, add some water slowly and stir to make it smooth. Store bought roux can be substituted for the homemade if preferred.

Sauté:
1 onion, chopped
1 bell pepper, chopped
Celery, chopped (about the same amount as onion and bell pepper)
3 to 4 cloves garlic, chopped

Add sautéed vegetables to roux and water and bring to a boil. At this point you will know how much more water to add for desired consistency. Cook until vegetables are tender.

This is the basis for all types of gumbo. Follow the Chicken Gumbo recipe on page 60, or use other ingredients or a combination of them to make Chicken & Sausage Gumbo, Shrimp Gumbo, Shrimp & Crab Gumbo or Seafood Gumbo. Most ingredients are interchangeable according to taste.

BAYOU BLEND

2 ribs celery, chopped
1 chopped bell pepper
1 chopped onion
1 clove garlic
1 stick margarine
1 can cream of mushroom soup
10 ounces grated sharp cheese
2½ cups cooked rice
1 pound cleaned and de-veined raw shrimp
1 pound crab meat
Salt and pepper to taste
Feel free to add a little red pepper as it makes Cajun food taste more Cajun.

Steam shrimp in 1 cup of water and keep the broth. Melt margarine in skillet and sauté celery, bell pepper, onion and garlic over low heat. When transparent add cooked rice, cream of mushroom soup, half the cheese (reserve other half for top), shrimp, crab meat and reserved broth from shrimp. Season to taste with salt and pepper. Cook on top of stove for a few minutes. Pour in 9 x 13 pan (sprayed with Pam) and top with remaining cheese. Bake at 375°F for 50 minutes.

CAJUN GUMBO FOR TEXANS
By Joan T. Hollier

I use 5 to 6 chicken legs for gumbo because dark meat has better flavor, but you can use any chicken. Skin and defat the chicken and boil it until tender. Cool and remove bones from meat. I often do this process ahead of time and freeze the meat and stock separately for when I make gumbo.

I use a gumbo base—Zatarains and Bayou Magic are my favorites, but there are others available at HEB, Fiesta and other stores. Some brands include rice, but I prefer the kind without rice. Dissolve gumbo base in cold water and add the stock you previously made. Stir until it boils, and simmer while preparing the next step. Never boil gumbo, simmer gently at all stages.

When I can get fresh okra, I chop it and spread it on an oiled tray in a 350°F oven, stirring occasionally until wilted, about 25 to 30 minutes. I prepare ahead and freeze for later use. You can get 2 pound packages frozen at Fiesta, and one package is enough for a gumbo for 6 to 8 people. Gumbo can also be made without okra.

I use 2 to 4 large onions and 5 to 6 ribs of celery, chopped. Sauté in cooking oil until soft and add to stock and gumbo base. Add the okra and simmer 20 to 30 minutes.

Add ½ pound sausage cut in 1" pieces. Simmer until sausage is done.

Add the chicken meat last, as it is already cooked. Simmer 15 to 20 minutes. Add 1 bunch green onions and ½ bunch parsley, chopped.

The gumbo base already has the roux and the seasonings in it, but I sometimes add basil, and I always add red pepper and Tabasco or other hot sauce.

Gumbo is best if prepared ahead and left to mellow in the pot for a couple of hours. Heat again but do not boil. Serve over rice. I serve over rice even if the gumbo base had rice in it. A Cajun, even a Texas Cajun, can't get too much rice. Ummmn Good!!
Gumbo freezes well.

—Joan T. Hollier writes book reviews, features, and travel articles. Her column *RV With Me* appears regularly in the *Williamson County Sun*. After living 13 years in New Orleans, she and her Cajun husband, Rusty, moved to Georgetown, discovering that retirement mecca before Sun City. You should taste her crawfish etouffé!

CAJUN JAMBALAYA
By Jeanette Robinson

6 slices bacon, cut into bite size pieces
1 cup chopped celery
1 chopped onion
1 green bell pepper, seed and chop
½ pound smoked sausage, cut into bite size pieces
½ pound cooked ham, cut into bite size pieces
½ pound cooked chicken, cut into bite size pieces
2 - 14.5 ounce cans crushed tomatoes (undrained)
2 cups chicken broth
2 cups beef broth
1 teaspoon dried thyme
2 ¼ teaspoons Cajun Seasoning
2 cups uncooked rice
½ pound of the tiny salad shrimp

Directions: Heat a large pot or Dutch oven over medium high heat. When hot, add bacon and cook until crispy. Remove bacon and set aside, reserving bacon grease in pot. Add celery, green bell pepper and onion to bacon grease and cook until tender.

Add the ham, chicken and sausage and pour in tomatoes, beef and chicken broth. Season with thyme and Cajun seasoning. Bring to boil, add rice, return to boil. Turn to low heat, cover and simmer for 20 minutes or until rice is tender.

Stir in shrimp and bacon just before serving and heat through. If shrimp was uncooked, let it cook for about five minutes before serving.

CHEESE BUTTON CASSEROLE
By Mary Pollock

16 ounces Bow Tie pasta, cooked
1 quart cottage cheese
1 cup sour cream
2 bunches chopped green onions
2 teaspoons salt
1 egg + ¾ cup milk, beaten together
1 cube butter divided in half
Bread cubes

Sauté green onions in butter. Mix with sour cream, cottage cheese and salt. Layer: Pasta, cheese mixture, pasta, cheese mixture, etc. Pour egg/milk mixture over top. Brown bread cubes in butter. Place on top of casserole Bake at 350°F for 1 hour.

CHEESE ENCHILADAS
By Anissa Russell

Family Tidbit: This is my son Michael's all-time ultimate superior above all favorite! That is just putting it mildly. I can always count on getting a hug from Michael when I cook him up some enchiladas. How does the saying go? The way to a man's heart is through his stomach. If you are used to Tex-Mex enchiladas these might be a shock for you. These are true authentic enchiladas, not like the ones you get in a lot of Mexican Restaurants. Of course, when you get used to the real enchiladas you cannot go back.

1 large bag of New Mexico Chili pods
4 large cans of Tomato Sauce
Corn Tortillas
Oil
Muenster Cheese (or your favorite)
Garlic Powder
Salt
Red Pepper, optional

Boil whole bag of chili pods in large pot until tender. Once tender and cool to touch, pull off stems. Put 5 or 6 chilies in a blender with a can of tomato sauce. Once blended, pour into a strainer over a large bowl.

Strain until no more liquid falls through. Throw away what is left in the strainer (which is the skin and seeds.) Continue to process until all chili pods are blended.

Add salt and garlic powder to taste.

Sometimes I add a little red pepper if the chilies are not hot enough (Michael and I like ours spicy).

Heat about ¼ cup of oil in skillet on high. Once hot, reduce heat to medium, dip corn tortilla in sauce and fry in hot oil until tender, flipping once. Remove tortilla from skillet and lay on plate. Add cheese and roll up tortilla. Continue the process until as many enchiladas are cooked that you want to eat. Refrigerate remaining sauce for next time. Great served with a dollop of sour cream on top.

Also try the meat enchiladas variation.

CHICKEN GUMBO

Boil chicken, remove from broth, debone and add to gumbo. Use the chicken stock in place of part of the water in the gumbo. If desired, sausage can be added for additional flavor. When adding sausage, I prefer to cook some of the grease out before adding to gumbo mixture.

Shrimp, crab or other seafood: Add to gumbo. Cook for 30 minutes.

The rest of the seasonings are added to taste: Salt, black pepper, red pepper, Nature's Seasoning, Creole or Cajun Seasoning. Some of these can be pretty spicy so taste often to check for flavor.

Chopped green onions and okra can be added during the last 15 minutes. I like to chop green onion and have in small bowl to sprinkle on gumbo at the table.

Serve with rice, potato salad, crackers, and gumbo file.

CHICKEN SOUP EXTRAORDINAIRE

1 can chicken broth
2 stalks celery, chopped
2 carrots, chopped
1 small onion, chopped
1 clove garlic, chopped
3 potatoes, cubed
2 whole boneless chicken breasts, cubed
½ cup water
1 small can greens peas, undrained
Small amount of chopped broccoli

Put all of above in a large pot and cook slowly. When almost done, lower heat and add:
1 small package of Velveeta cheese
1 can cream of chicken soup

CHICKEN TETRAZINI

4 to 5 chicken breasts cut in small pieces
1 teaspoon onion salt
½ teaspoon celery salt
½ pound thin spaghetti
½ cup chopped mushrooms
1 chopped onion
½ cup chopped bell pepper
6 Tablespoons butter
2 Tablespoons flour
¼ teaspoon black pepper
¼ cup cooking sherry or cooking white wine
1 can chicken broth
1 cup heavy cream
¾ pound Velveeta cheese cut in small cubes
1 cup grated Cheddar cheese
1 cup breadcrumbs

Cook chicken until tender in water seasoned with onion and celery salt. Remove and let cool. Reserve chicken broth. Add water to remaining broth and cook spaghetti. Sauté mushrooms, onion and bell pepper in 3 Tablespoons butter. Combine with 3 Tablespoons butter, flour, pepper, sherry/white wine and Swanson's chicken broth in large pot. Heat and stir till thickened. Add cream and then mix well. Add spaghetti and chicken and mix well. Add Velveeta and stir until melted. Pour into 9 x 13 oiled baking dish. Top with cheddar cheese and sprinkle breadcrumbs evenly on top.

Bake at 400°F for 30 minutes until bubbly.
Serves 8.

CHILI TAMALE CASSEROLE

Tortilla Chips
Small can of tamales cut into small pieces
1 can of chili
1 can of refried beans
1/8 cup chopped onions, sautéed
Shredded cheddar or pepper jack cheese

Crumble enough tortilla chips to lightly cover bottom of casserole dish. Add tamale pieces. Heat chili and refried beans and mix together. Add onions. Pour this mixture over tamales. Top with cheese.

Bake in oven for 30 minutes at 350°F—or cook in microwave oven for 5 to 7 minutes until cheese is melted and all is heated well.

Serves 4.

CHIPOLTE BURGERS
By Anissa Russell

These can be spicy!

1 can chipotle peppers in adobo sauce, undrained
2 pounds lean ground beef
Steak seasoning
Cheddar cheese cut into small slices

Process the chipotle peppers in a blender till smooth. Combine a few teaspoons of the puree chipotle—the more you add the spicier it gets—and steak seasoning, about 2 Tablespoons, to the ground beef. Mix well but do not over mix.

Shape about half the meat into patties and put the cheddar cheese slices in the middle. Shape the rest of the patties and put on top of thecheese and shape together, sealing the edges. Seal good so thecheese does not melt out while grilling. When close to finishing top with additional cheese. For a real spice treat use chipotle cheddar sliced cheese.

CORNBREAD DRESSING
By Sheri Bethard

2 cups cornmeal
½ cup self-rising flour
2 teaspoons baking powder
1 teaspoon baking soda
1 teaspoon salt
2 eggs, beaten
2 cups buttermilk
2 Tablespoons bacon drippings, melted, or olive oil

Combine first 5 ingredients in a large mixing bowl; add next 3 ingredients and mix well.

Place a well-greased 10 inch cast iron skillet in a 450°F oven for 4 minutes or until hot. Remove from oven; spoon batter into pan.

Bake at 450°F for 35 minutes or until lightly browned. Cool; crumble cornbread into a large bowl.

3 stalks celery, chopped
1 medium onion, chopped
1 leek, chopped (optional)
4 green onions, chopped (optional)
2 Tablespoons butter or margarine
2 ½ cups chicken broth (low sodium)
1 ½ cups milk
2 eggs, beaten
1 teaspoon salt
1 teaspoon poultry seasoning
¾ teaspoon pepper
½ cup herbed breadcrumbs
¼ cup parsley flakes

Sauté celery and onion in butter until tender. Combine cornbread, sautéed vegetables, and remaining ingredients, mixing well. Spoon into a lightly greased 13 x 9x 2 inch baking pan.

Bake at 450°F for 25 to 30 minutes.

Yield 8 servings.

CRAWFISH CORNBREAD

2 eggs
1 teaspoon salt
1 teaspoon baking soda
1 medium onion, chopped
½ cup yellow cornmeal
1½ cups grated cheddar cheese, divided
¼ to ½ cup chopped jalapenos
1 can cream style corn
1 pound crawfish tails

Mix all ingredients together, saving out ½ cup cheese.

Place in an 8x13 inch greased loaf pan or casserole dish. Bake 30 to 40 minutes at 375°F. Sprinkle ½ cup grated cheese on top just before removing from the oven. Serve as a main dish, not as bread.

CRAWFISH ETOUFFE

2 pounds crawfish
2 cups chopped onions
1 cup chopped celery
1 cup chopped bell pepper
2 cloves garlic
½ cup butter
½ cup chopped green onion tops
1 can Rotel tomatoes
1 can cream of mushroom soup
1 small jar mushrooms, drained
½ cup chopped parsley
Tony Chachere's Creole Seasoning

DO NOT ADD SALT before tasting. The ingredients are already salty.

Sauté onions, celery and bell peppers until clear, then add garlic. Add tomatoes, cream of mushroom soup and drained mushrooms; stir well. Add drained crawfish.

Cook slowly about 20 minutes. Add parsley and onion tops and cook 10 more minutes. Serve over hot rice. Sprinkle each dish with an additional spoonful of chopped green onion tops.

CRAWFISH PIE
By Flo Cormier

¾ medium bell pepper
1 large onion, chopped
2 celery ribs, chopped
¾ cup butter
6 Tablespoons crawfish fat

½ cup chopped green onion
1½ pounds peeled crawfish tails
½ cup minced parsley
1½ teaspoons salt
½ teaspoon black pepper
1/8 teaspoon red pepper
½ teaspoon garlic powder
Cornstarch
Dough for a double pie crust (see recipe below)

Sauté bell pepper, onion and celery in butter until tender. Add crawfish fat and simmer 10 minutes. Add crawfish tails, green onion, parsley and seasonings. Thicken if necessary with cornstarch; let cook long enough to thicken gravy. Place half of the pie dough in a 9-inch pie pan. Fill with the cooled crawfish filling. Place top crust on pie, moisten and seal edges. Cut 2 inch-long slits in the top of crust. Bake for 10 minutes at 450°F. Lower oven to 375°F and cook for about 35 minutes longer or until crust is golden brown.

Pastry for Pie Shell:
1¼ cups sifted all-purpose flour
½ teaspoon salt
½ cup margarine
2½ Tablespoons cold milk

Sift flour and salt in a mixing bowl. Add ½ cup margarine. Cut the margarine into the flour. Sprinkle 2½ Tablespoons cold milk over the mixture. Beat at low speed, scraping sides and bottom of bowl. Beat until all particles cling together. Roll out on floured board. Prepared refrigerated pie crust may be substituted for home made crust.

CRAWFISH SOUP
By Glenda Dickey

4 cloves of garlic
1 large onion, chopped
½ stick of butter
1 can cream corn
1 can mushroom soup
1 can potato soup
2 cups water mixed with
2/3 cup dry potato soup mix (I use Bear Creek brand)
1 cup bell pepper, chopped
1 pound crawfish tail meat
1 pint Half & Half cream
2 stalks celery, chopped
Red Pepper to taste
Tony Chachere's Creole seasoning to taste

Do not salt until after tasting as soups are salty. Sauté onions, bell pepper and celery in butter. Add corn, soups, Half & Half cream and seasonings to taste. Add crawfish tails. Simmer 30 minutes. If too thick, add more Half & Half. In true southern style, serve with cornbread. Delicious!

EGGPLANT AND SHRIMP CASSEROLE

1 large eggplant
½ cup onion, chopped
½ cup celery, chopped
½ green pepper, chopped
½ cup plus 2 Tablespoons butter
½ cup flour
½ teaspoon salt
¼ teaspoon black pepper
1 cup rich milk (or cream)
1 cup shrimp (canned or fresh)
1 egg
1 cup bread crumbs
2 Tablespoons Parmesan cheese, grated

Pare eggplant and cut into 1 inch cubes. Cook in salted water until tender, drain. Place in a 2 quart casserole. Cook onion, celery, and green pepper in ¼ cup butter until soft, but not browned; blend in flour, salt, black pepper. Stir in milk and shrimp. Cook until thickened, stirring constantly. Quickly stir in egg then spoon mixture over eggplant. Top with crumbs coasted with remaining butter and cheese.

Bake at 375°F for 25 to 35 minutes until brown.

Yield 6 servings.

FRIED CATFISH

If you are going to cook "southern" you must be able to fry up a good mess of catfish! The percentage of each ingredient, below, is used according to taste.

Catfish
Yellow corn meal
Oil
Red Pepper
Cajun Seasoning
Salt and Pepper

Mix cornmeal, red pepper and Cajun seasoning, or you can use just salt and pepper instead depending on your seasoning preferences. Roll catfish in the cornmeal and fry in hot oil until crispy. Serve with raw sliced onions or green onions.

Fried Shrimp and Catfish

Recipes on pages 70 and 72

FRIED SHRIMP
By Ruth Dickey

This recipe is not an exact science, but Ruth always made the best fried shrimp. You will have to play with it yourself to determine what spices you like the best, but listed below are the basics. Of course, shrimp right off the gulf is best!

Peeled deveined shrimp (as much as you need)
Flour
Salt
Baking powder
Creole Seasoning
Black Pepper

In a bowl large enough to hold the cleaned, deveined shrimp, add two or three eggs and approximately ¼ cup of milk. Mix well. Add the shrimp and mix, making sure the shrimp are all coated well. On a plate, mix the flour, salt, baking powder, Creole seasoning and black pepper. Heat cooking oil in a large skillet on medium high heat. Take egg coated shrimp, and, one by one, roll them in the flour mixture until they are well coated. Drop each in the hot oil. Cook for approximately 2 to 3 minutes or until shrimp are done. It usually doesn't take shrimp long to cook. Serve hot.

GRILLADES
—New Orleans style smothered steak—
Recipe adapted from Grandma Rosalie Rogers

2 pounds Sirloin steak, ½ inch thick, cut into bite size pieces
1 bunch green onions, chopped
1 cup medium white onion, chopped
1 cup chopped celery
2 cloves garlic, minced
1 teaspoon seasoned salt
1 teaspoon seasoned pepper
1 Tablespoon flour
2 Tablespoons olive oil
1 teaspoon garlic salt
1 ½ cups red cooking wine
1 - 14.5 ounce can diced tomatoes (roasted garlic or any other flavor, by Hunts)
3 to 4 cups water
3 to 4 bay leaves
3 Tablespoons parsley
Kitchen Bouquet if needed for darkening of gravy

Brown both sides of meat in the oil. Remove and set aside for the time being. Add flour to drippings and cook until dark brown over low heat to make a dark roux. Add onions and celery, cook until tender, then add tomatoes. Cook for about 5 minutes. Add all ingredients except for the meat and parsley and bring to a simmer. Now add meat and simmer for 2 hours or longer. Add water as needed to keep meat covered or until meat is tender. About 15 minutes before ready to serve add parsley and stir in. The longer it's cooked the better the taste.

If you allow the grillades to sit for several hours or overnight in the refrigerator, reheating improves the taste.

I DON'T KNOW
By Sheri Bethard

One evening while browning ground round my children asked me what I was making for supper. I told them at the time, "I don't know." I started adding various ingredients and this was the result. So, from then on they would ask for "I don't know" for supper and still today they ask for it and have shared the recipe with their friends.

1 to 1 ½ pounds of ground round
½ onion, chopped
4 green onions, chopped
½ bell pepper, chopped
4 garlic cloves, minced

Brown meat, add onions & peppers while browning. Drain grease.

Add:
1 can corn, drained
1 package taco seasoning
1 cup water
1 can cheddar cheese soup
onion powder
garlic powder
salt
pepper

Mix together and simmer 15 to 20 minutes. Add seasonings to taste. Serves: 6 to 8.

* For a spicier version add one can of diced spicy Mexican style tomatoes.

MEAT ENCHILADAS
By Anissa Russell

1 large bag of New Mexico Chili pods
4 large cans of Tomato Sauce
Corn Tortillas
Oil
Ground Meat
Chili Powder
Red Pepper
Cumin
Salt and Pepper
Parsley
Garlic Powder

Cook meat until browned. Remove grease. Add enough water to float meat.

Add seasonings to taste and simmer until the water evaporates.

Prepare the chilies and cook the tortillas following the directions in the Cheese Enchiladas recipe.

Add meat and cheese to tortillas and roll up. Don't forget to add a dollop of sour cream as desired.

RUSS' CHILI: A WORK IN PROGRESS
By Russell Hogg

I have been experimenting with chili since I first learned the basics from Mom. This is my current incarnation: But before I begin, let me give a word to the wise. When buying chili powder, avoid the cheap brands. It makes no sense, to my mind, to buy a cheap chili powder and use two to three times as much to get the right flavor. Even with a good brand of chili powder, you should be using at least 3 Tablespoons.

2 pounds ground beef, turkey, or pork
1 - 16 ounce can crushed or diced tomatoes, with juice
2 to 3 cans of beans, rinsed (use beans of choice)
Dried chilies. (I use 2 to 3 Ancho and 2 to 3 New Mexico Chiles)
1 to 2 fresh chilies, chopped finely—my favorite is Poblano
1 large onion, chopped finely
4 to 5 cloves of garlic, chopped finely
Cayenne pepper to taste
Louisiana hot sauce to taste
Chili powder to taste

1 cup water; more water may be added later for desired consistency.
½ to 1 cup dark beer. The darker the better—I recommend Spaaten Optimator.
Salt and pepper, to taste.

In the morning wash all the dried peppers and put them in a bowl of water, 1 cup or so, and refrigerate to rehydrate. After a few hours, they should be soft, and the water should have turned a rich red color. From here you have two options: mince up the chilies or put the whole mixture in the blender. Either way works, but be sure to save both water and chilies.

Brown the ground meat in a large pot; drain any grease, then add one half of the chopped onion and one half of the garlic. Several minutes later, add the chopped fresh chilies. Cook, stirring regularly until onions begin to appear translucent. Add can of tomatoes, then add the Chile-Water mixture. Bring to a boil and simmer for a few minutes, at which time you should add the remaining onion and garlic, and the beans. Add spices and hot sauce, being sure to taste after each adjustment. Be liberal with your chili powder.

When the mixture is to your liking, simmer on low heat stirring occasionally, and adding water to keep the consistency right. If you've made it too spicy, a little sugar will help cut that back. Several hours is best, but a half hour will do okay. Half an hour before serving add the beer and stir. For serving, it's best to sprinkle liberally with cheese. Cornbread and/or Fritos are a very nice accompaniment.

Author's note: A dollop of sour cream on top can help *soothe the savage beast.*

SEAFOOD CASSEROLE
By Ann Pence

1 stick butter
6 to 8 ounces sliced mushrooms, drained
½ cup celery, chopped
½ cup onion, chopped
½ cup bell pepper, chopped
1 tall can salmon, drained, bones removed
1 can crab meat, drained
* The seafood above may be substituted with shrimp and/or tuna
1 or 2 cans of green beans, drained
1 can Water Chestnuts, drained
2 ½ cups Mayonnaise (Real Mayo)
3 to 4 teaspoons Creole Mustard
3 teaspoons Worcestershire Sauce
2 ½ or 3 cups bread crumbs (Italian flavored are good)

Sauté mushrooms, celery, onion, and bell pepper in butter until tender.

In large bowl, mix all ingredients, except bread crumbs.

Put into casserole dish and top with bread crumbs. Shredded cheese may be put on top also.

Bake 350°F for 35 to 45 minutes, until hot. Serve warm or you may refrigerate and serve cold.

SMOTHERED CHICKEN
By Tommye Johnson

1 - 2 to 3 pound chicken, cut into pieces
2 Tablespoons soy sauce
Salt to taste
Louisiana hot sauce or ground cayenne pepper to taste
2 Tablespoons oil
2 cups chopped onion
½ cup chopped bell pepper
½ cup chopped fresh parsley
1 cup dry white wine
2 teaspoons chopped garlic

Rinse the chicken well, pat dry, then season it with the soy sauce, salt, and hot sauce, and set aside. In a large, high-walled skillet, heat the oil, then sauté the onions, bell pepper, and parsley over medium-high heat until the onions are clear. Add the wine and stir; add garlic and stir, then add the chicken. Mix everything together, then lower the heat to medium, cover, and cook for at least 2 hours, stirring occasionally. The chicken should be so tender that it falls apart. Serve over cooked rice.

SOUTHERN FRIED CHICKEN

This is the real thing—and there's nothing like it for Sunday dinner or any other time. It was said best by one old timer, "Fried chicken is excellent hot, cold or at room temperature." Ain't it the truth?

>1 frying chicken cut into pieces
>½ cup Kosher salt
>8 cups water
>1 cup all-purpose flour
>2 Tablespoon cornstarch
>½ teaspoon Kosher salt
>1 teaspoon black pepper
>Peanut oil for frying

Dissolve ½ cup kosher salt in the 8 cups of water. Arrange chicken in a bowl large enough hold both chicken and the salt brine. Pour brine over chicken to cover it, cover bowl with plastic wrap and refrigerate 8 hours. Sift together the cornstarch, flour, the ½ teaspoon Kosher salt, and pepper. Heat 1 inch peanut oil over medium heat in cast iron skillet until water drops sizzle across the surface. Drain brine from chicken, dredge pieces in flour mixture and fry in hot oil until golden brown and cooked through.

ANOTHER VERSION OF SOUTHERN FRIED CHICKEN
By Mary Miller

1 chicken, cut up, or equivalent
Flour
Pancake mix
Milk
Salt and pepper

Mix flour, salt and pepper together.

In separate dish, mix pancake mix and milk to make a thin batter.

Dip chicken in batter, then coat with flour mixture. Fry in hot oil until done and brown.

SEAFOOD STUFFED CHINESE CABBAGE
By Johnnie Doris Jones

- 1 cup diced fish (preferably red fish)
- 1 cup diced shrimp (fresh)
- 1 cup diced fresh tomato
- 1/2 cup diced onion
- 1/4 cup diced bell pepper
- 1 Tablespoon parsley flakes
- ½ teaspoon garlic powder
- 1 teaspoon chives
- ½ teaspoon red pepper
- 1 teaspoon lemon pepper
- 2 Tablespoons fish sauce or soy sauce
- 2 Tablespoons melted butter or margarine

Mix all ingredients together thoroughly and set aside. Wilt cabbage leaves in hot water. Put ¼ cup mixture in each cabbage leaf. Secure with toothpicks and place in electric skillet to steam. Top cabbage rolls with 1 diced tomato, ¼ cup chopped bell pepper, ¼ cup chopped onion. Pour in 1 cup water and cover. Heat to boiling and reduce heat to simmer for 1 hour.

Approximately 90 calories per serving.
Serves 6 to 8.

TEXAS BARBEQUE DAMMIT
Third generation recipe

1 bottle ketchup
1 can tomato sauce (small)
1 tomato sauce can water
1 lemon, sliced, squeezed and dropped in
1/3 cup vinegar
Pepper sauce
3 Tablespoons Worcestershire sauce
4 cloves garlic
1 stick butter
2 teaspoons black pepper
¼ teaspoon cayenne pepper
1 large onion, chopped
1 Tablespoon Louisiana Red Hot Sauce
Salt to taste
1 Tablespoon brown sugar

Can also use molasses or cane syrup instead of brown sugar; liquid smoke also adds a nice touch, and I tend to use more vinegar than the recipe calls for (and Worcestershire sauce, sometimes). You should be able to use only tomato sauce (no ketchup) if you increase the vinegar, sugar, etc. Remove lemon parts after it's cooked for 20 to 30 minutes, then liquefy everything in your blender/food processor if desired.

Use this sauce on Barbeque Ribs or your favorite meat.

BARBEQUE RIBS

Rack of pork ribs. You can use two or three racks, as desired

Clean each rack. Pat dry and rub with coarse ground pepper and coarse salt. Wrap tightly in aluminum foil. Par bake at 250°F for two hours.

Unwrap and put on hot grill, coat with Texas Barbeque Dammit sauce, or you favorite sauce, and grill until desired brown color. Enjoy!

"WRIGHT" STEW
By Renée Johnson

Assemble in large Crock Pot

1 bag frozen meatballs
1 can black beans
1 can lima beans
1 cup diced carrots
1/3 cup chopped parsley
2 large tomatoes, diced small
4 ribs celery, diced
Pinch of rosemary
Pinch of thyme
4 cups water (beef broth makes it even better)
2 cloves minced fresh garlic
Salt and pepper to taste

Cook in Crock Pot set on high for five hours. Delicious served with homemade cornbread.

Recipe on page 98

VEGETABLES

"Them gals are like two peas in a pod."

Recipe on page 96

AUNT ANNIE'S CORN PATTIES

1 can cream style corn
1 egg, beaten
1½ teaspoons baking powder
1 Tablespoon sugar
1½ cups flour
Dash of salt

Mix all ingredients together and stir well. Drop by tablespoon into hot cooking oil or shortening over medium heat. Fry until bubbles appear through the patties.

Use a slotted spoon or tongs to turn each patty over to brown on both sides. When brown, lift patties out of oil and place in a bowl lined with paper towels.

BROCCOLI SALAD

2 heads of broccoli, crowns only, coarsely chopped
1 pound bacon, fried crisp and crumbled
½ medium red onion, finely grated
16 ounces cheddar cheese, grated
1 cup mayonnaise
½ cup sugar
2 Tablespoons vinegar

In a large bowl, combine all the ingredients, stir and refrigerate until ready to serve. May be prepared in advance and kept in refrigerator.

CAJUN POTATO SALAD

8 cups cooked potato cubes
5 hard-boiled eggs, chopped
1 cup dill pickle relish
½ cups chopped olives
1 cup chopped onion
½ cup chopped celery
2 cups mayonnaise
2 Tablespoons prepared mustard
Salt and pepper to taste
Louisiana hot sauce or cayenne pepper to taste

In a large bowl, combine above ingredients and serve. May be prepared in advance and refrigerated until the next day.

CHRISTMAS CARROTS

Blanch 2 pound bag of small carrots (or cut up whole ones) for 12 minutes, drain
Melt 3 Tablespoons butter in skillet
Add 4 shallots, sliced thin. Sauté until wilted
Add ¼ cup honey
½ teaspoon salt
Add: Blanched carrots and heat thoroughly

Beautiful served in a clear, cut glass bowl.

COLESLAW

1 head of cabbage, shredded
½ bell pepper, chopped or finely sliced
1 onion, shredded
1 cup sugar
Combine in large bowl or container and set aside
Prepare Dressing

Dressing:

Mix together in saucepan:
½ cup cider vinegar
½ cup vegetable oil
1 teaspoon salt
½ teaspoon mustard seed
½ teaspoon celery seed

Heat and pour over cabbage mixture. Refrigerate.

CORN CASSEROLE
By Margaret Morgan

Who doesn't love a good corn casserole? Margaret puts a little extra spice in her recipe with the jalapenos.

3 cans of shoepeg corn, drained
2 Tablespoons chopped jalapenos (can use green and red to add color)
1 to 2 Tablespoons jalapeno juice (from canned peppers)
1 stick butter
8 ounces cream cheese
¼ cup milk
Salt and pepper to taste

Cook butter, cream cheese, and milk until smooth and it begins to boil.

Add remaining ingredients, pour in a buttered casserole dish and bake at 350°F for 30 minutes.

EXTRA CRISPY CAJUN FRY BATTER
By Kathie Ruiz

If you wonder how those Cajuns do it, this is how!

Put 3 or 4 cups of flour in a gallon zipper bag.
Add any Cajun or Louisiana seasoning or make your own.

In a large bowl put 3 cups of buttermilk and 1 beaten egg.

Put whatever you are frying (onion rings, shrimp, meat) in the flour first, then into the buttermilk, then back into the flour.
Deep fry in hot oil until golden brown and extra crispy. Do not overload the pan so the temperature stays hot and food has room to crisp up. Drain on paper towels and serve hot.

FAMILY FAVORITE POTATO SALAD
By Sylvia Dickey Smith

Put desired number of potatoes in a large pot, cover with water, allowing room to boil 2-3 eggs along with the potatoes. Eggs may be taken out after ten minutes boiling time. When potatoes are fork tender, drain off water and allow to cool until ready to make the salad.

Peel potatoes, peel eggs, and chop all into a large bowl.

Add mayonnaise and mustard to potato/egg mixture to desired moist content, smashing hunks of potatoes as stirred. Add salt and pepper to taste. Refrigerate until ready to eat. Delicious. Even folks who don't like potato salad rave about this recipe.

FRIED GREEN TOMATOES

¼ cup flour
2 egg whites, stiffly beaten
2 teaspoons ranch buttermilk dressing mix
½ cup breadcrumbs or cornmeal
3 green tomatoes, sliced in ¼ inch thick pieces
Oil, for frying

Put flour and either breadcrumbs or cornmeal in two separate shallow dishes and set aside. Combine egg whites and dry buttermilk mix and set aside. Coat each tomato slice with flour and dip in egg mixture then in breadcrumbs. Cook in hot oil a few minutes each side. Sprinkle with fresh parmesan.

FRIED OKRA

1 pound fresh okra
1 cup flour
1 cup cracker meal
1½ teaspoons salt, divided
½ teaspoon pepper
1 egg
1 cup buttermilk
Enough oil to fry

Wash okra, drain. Cut off tips and stem ends; cut okra crosswise into ½ inch slices. Combine flour, cracker meal, 1 teaspoon salt, and pepper in shallow dish. Combine egg, buttermilk, and remaining ½ teaspoon salt in a dish, mixing well. Add about 1/3 of okra to egg mixture, then remove okra with a slotted spoon, and place in flour mixture, stirring gently to coat okra. Pour oil to depth of 2 inches into an iron skillet, heat to 375°F. Fry okra until golden brown. Drain well on paper towels. Continue process with remaining okra. Serve hot. Sliced yellow squash or zucchini can be substituted for the okra if desired.

ONION PIE

Mouth-watering delicious! Christmas or Thanksgiving is not the same without it.

1 cup salted cracker crumbs (Ritz)
¼ cup melted butter
2 to 3 medium onions, sliced
¼ cup melted butter
½ cup grated Sharp Cheddar cheese—be sure to use sharp cheddar, it makes a difference
4 eggs
1 cup Half & Half or milk (your preference)
Salt and pepper to taste

Toss cracker crumbs and first ¼ cup melted butter, press into bottom sides of pie plate. Cook sliced onions over low heat in second ¼ cup butter till tender and caramelized (this is the secret to the best pie). Place onions in cracker crust. Beat eggs slightly, add milk slowly with salt and pepper and pour over onions. Sprinkle with cheese. Bake at 350°F for 25 minutes, or until slightly browned.

PINTO BEANS AND MORE
By Jane Gunlock

¾ medium package of pinto beans (dried)
1 pound ground meat
1 package taco seasoning mix
1 - 14.5 ounce can stewed tomatoes (diced)
1 - 8 ounce can tomato sauce
Salt pork or bacon
Garlic salt
Dash of chili powder
Parsley flakes to taste
Salt and pepper to taste

Sauté ground meat and drain. Add taco mix and a small amount of water. Cook until well blended. Set aside. Wash beans well and place in slow cooker. Add salt pork or bacon, then water to reach within an inch of so from top of cooker. Cook beans on high until tender. Discard salt pork, if used. Add cooked ground meat, tomatoes, tomato sauce, and dry ingredients. Continue to cook on high until all ingredients are combined well.

RED GRAPE & BROCCOLI SALAD
By Helen Williams

4 cups red grapes - 1-1/2 pounds
4 cups broccoli - tips only cut into small pieces (save stems for soup or vegetable dish)
1 cup celery chopped fine
1 bunch green onions chopped fine
½ cup sliced almonds
6 slices bacon - crumble

Dressing:
1 cup Kraft's low cholesterol-fat free mayo
¼ cup sugar
4 teaspoons lemon juice

Mix top 6 ingredients and then combine with dressing. Best flavor achieved if allowed to set overnight before serving.

SOUTHERN SWEET POTATO CRISP

2 cups shredded sweet potatoes (love that food processor)
1 cup sugar
½ cup milk
2 eggs
1 stick melted butter
1 teaspoon vanilla

Cream butter and sugar. Add eggs, milk and mix. Stir in shredded sweet potatoes.

Rub butter all around sides and bottom of casserole dish 11 x 9 inch (makes a thin layer).

Bake at 350°F 45 minutes or until the tops and edges are brownish-colored.

SWEET POTATO CASSEROLE
By Sheri Bethard

2 large cans of sweet potatoes
1 cup brown sugar
¼ cup milk
½ cup butter, softened
2 large eggs
1 teaspoon vanilla extract
¼ teaspoon salt
1 cup miniature marshmallows

Cook sweet potatoes in juice until tender. Mash sweet potatoes. Beat mashed sweet potatoes, sugar, and next 5 ingredients at medium speed with an electric mixer until smooth. Spoon potato mixture into a greased 11x7 inch baking dish.

Pecan Topping

1 cup pecans chopped fine
½ cup brown sugar
½ cup all purpose flour
½ teaspoon ground cinnamon
½ cup butter at room temperature

Combine flour, brown sugar and ground cinnamon in medium bowl. Add butter and cut in until mixture resembles coarse crumbs. Mix in pecans.

Sprinkle marshmallows and pecan topping diagonally over casserole. Bake at 350°F for 30 minutes. Remove from oven, let stand 10 minutes before serving.

Serves 6 to 8.

SWISS CHARD & WHITE BEANS

2 bundles Swiss chard, washed and chopped (may use red or green chard)
2 to 3 cloves minced garlic
2 cups chicken stock (water may be substituted but stock gives a better flavor)
1 can Cannellini beans, rinsed
2 Tablespoons olive oil

In large pot, add oil and heat until medium hot. Add garlic and chard, sautéing until tender. Add chicken stock and simmer until tender. Add salt and pepper as desired. When done, add Cannellini beans and heat through.

Serve with a loaf of rustic bread. Delicious. This recipe can be made ahead, refrigerated and reheated.

TAMALE MASHED POTATOES

Boil, mash and prepare mashed potatoes as normal, adding butter, milk, salt, and pepper as desired. When done, break hot tamales (number related to quantity of mashed potatoes) into bite-size chunks and stir in with the potatoes and serve as usual. Delicious! Great with roast pork.

BONUS RECIPE

Last, but not least…

SIDRA SMART'S SASSY PICKLES

2 - 32 ounce jars thin-sliced hamburger dills, drained
4 cups sugar
½ teaspoon red pepper flakes
2 teaspoons Tabasco hot sauce
3 cloves garlic, minced

Sidra uses dried minced garlic. Instead of measuring, she dumps in as much as she likes, and she likes garlic! Also, the amounts of red pepper flakes and hot sauce can be modified to increase or lessen the heat.

Drain pickles well. Mix all ingredients together in large bowl. Stir every 30 minutes for 2 hours. Put pickles back in jars and refrigerate.

Sidra goes the extra mile for her pickles, however. She buys canning jars and lids, scalds them, and after adding pickles she gives them a hot water bath to seal.

About the Author

Award-winning mystery author Sylvia Dickey Smith, although a native of Orange, Texas, has lived from one side of the state to the other, with a few years in-between spent on the Caribbean island of Trinidad, W. I. She has spent time in mental hospitals and leper colonies (just visiting!), explored shell mounds of the Atakapa Indians, and trekked across alligator-infested swamp, all in the name of research. Prior to writing mysteries, she worked as a Licensed Professional Counselor and Marriage & Family Therapist, as well as a regional director in long term care programs. She currently lives in Georgetown, Texas with her husband, a retired Army Colonel.

Several recipes in this book are inspired by characters in Sylvia's Sidra Smart Mystery Series:

Dance on His Grave – ISBN 978-1-60318-006-1
Deadly Sins-Deadly Secrets – ISBN 978-1-60318-018-4
Dead Wreckoning – ISBN 978-1-60318-138-9

Learn more about Sylvia and her books at:
www.sylviadickeysmith.com

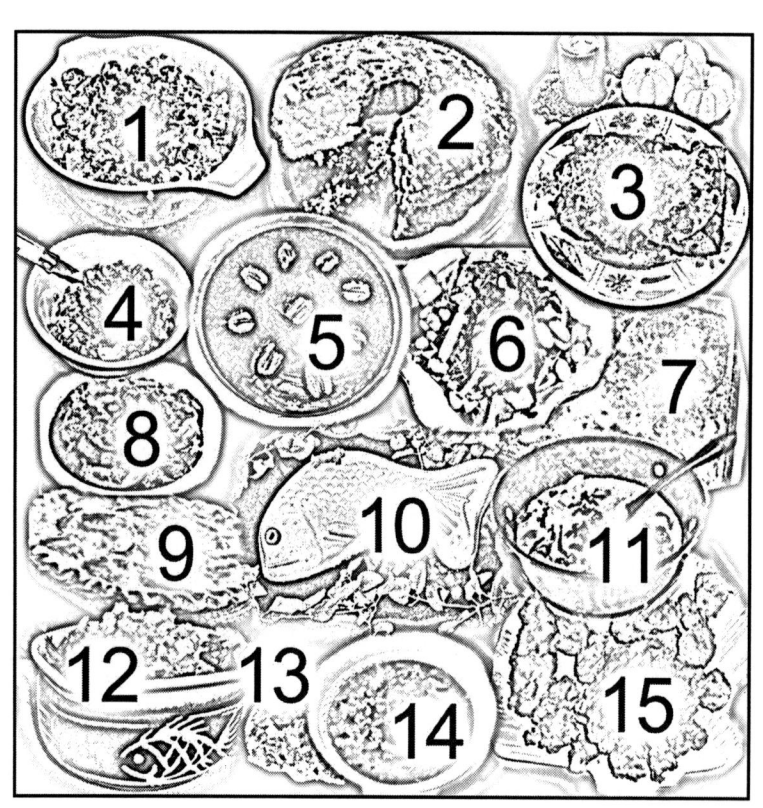

Shown on the back cover:

1 – Red Grape and Broccoli Salad
2 – Southern Hot Milk Cake
3 – Meat Enchiladas
4 – Russ' Granola
5 – No Fail Fudge
6 – Swiss Chard and White Beans
7 – Apple Cornbread
8 – Shrimp Gumbo
9 – Crawfish Pie
10 – Shrimp Mold
11 – Chicken & Dumplings
12 – Family Favorite Potato Salad
13 – Crawfish Cornbread
14 – Gumbo
15 – Fried Shrimp and Catfish

LaVergne, TN USA
14 September 2010
196884LV00004B/34/P